An Anthology Of The Collected poems

Imtiyaz Gull

ISBN 978-93-5559-149-4

Published in India 2022 by Pencil

A brand of
One Point Six Technologies Pvt. Ltd.
123, Building J2, Shram Seva Premises,
Wadala Truck Terminal, Wadala (E)
Mumbai 400037, Maharashtra, INDIA
E connect@thepencilapp.com
W www.thepencilapp.com

Author biography

Imtiyaz Gull, hails from a small hamlet Khuri Batapora(Noorabad) Kulgam. He is an english literature student & one of the finest younger author. He has been writing since 2017 and he is the coauthor of several international anthologies: Peace and poetry, Find me in my Rhymes, Melancholic Midnights, Colourful Thoughts and Words With Wings. He is also a coauthor of 'Litlight global illuminating literature e-magazine. He is really a passionate & portraying his feelings through his words. His favourite poets are Ghulam Ahmad Mehjoor, Alama Iqbal, Agha Shahid Ali & John Donne.

CONTENTS

Epigraph

Kashmir is my Elegy and I am 'HER' Poet

___Imtiyaz Gull

Foreword

It's a book that embraces all emotions, and the joy of expressing them in the act of writing. Many of these poems are painful to read but they still made me smile with recognition. It's a comforting thing to see yourself reflected on the page. It does exactly what good poetry does best - reflects your own unique experience whilst speaking universal truths.
Throughout the book, what shines brightest is a genuine, generous and inspirational faith in the act of reading and writing, how it carries us through the hardest times, how close it is to love."

It also provides a coverage of nostalgia like love, peace & harmony. This book contains poems that are in conversion with one another. Unified by theme, style, metaphors, Similes, choice of poetic form, and placed in a meticulous and deliberate order. In this very book, the poet has written on different genres. For instance; on Kashmir beauty, women molestation, Social issue, feminism & mothers unconditional love. He has portraying his feelings very well. In nutshell, this book is worth to read!

Sarbari Haldar Dasgupta,

Sanskrit Teacher.

Preface

I believe that most people have little trouble reading a poem, that most people like poetry, that most people crave the pure pleasure of poems, and that most people want a poem that's not too obvious. This book, "An Anthology Of The Collected Poems" provides a coverage of patriotism, nostalgia, unconditional love, peace and harmony.Its an interesting anthology & I have also written some Limerick poems and sonnets. And you enjoy this anthology. In preparing this anthology I have been helped by many colleagues, especially Mudasir Ahmad Thoker Sir and Sarbari Haldar Dasgupta ma'm. I sincerely hope that the good readers will find the book interesting, and they will enjoy, appreciate & encourage me!

__Author

Acknowledgements

I would like to express my gratitude to my parents, colleagues & my teachers, especially Mr Mudasir Ahmad Thoker Sir for a grant that made possible the considerable work. And they were involved in the preparation of this anthology.

Introduction

This poetry book, "An Anthology Of The Collected Poems" provides a coverage of mother's unconditional love, Patriotism, love, peace and harmony. In this anthology you'll find some masterpiece write-ups. I sincerely hope that the good readers will find the book interesting.

Limerick-I Don't call me Bhaijaan

Girls call me bhaijaan,

But I am not Salman Khan,

My friends love me very much,

Because I am very rich!

And we went to the Azerbaijan!

By Imtiyaz Gull

Camping through the Noorabad Jungles

Camping through the Noorabad Jungles

It was the mid July,

The Kounsarnag trek I still remember,

The thought of going to the heaven!

I was with my friends,

On earth made me feel so excited!

We were in joy & delighted,

Our eyes filled with enthusiasm & hope!

We went to places like Chiranbal & kadelbal

At first night we stay at Chiranbal,

At night it got all quite,

Except the babbling brook.

And as I watch the sun,

Some birds have started ,

Singing their happy whistling tunes!

The sounds are echoed far & wide,

In the early morning bliss,

Nature imbues, taking away the Sky's blues!

When we woke up early morning,

We did wazu & pray a salah!

We took kahwa flavoured with almond & saffron

We start trekking on second day,

Through the valley of green meadows,

Colourful birds chirping in green forests!

Finally we reached to our dream place,

People call her Kounsarnag!

The lake welcomes us,

To take in the breathtaking beauty!

A glimpse of heaven revealed.

Sun rise blinking over the Kousarnag

Green meadows smile to the sun

Watching sunset over a cup of hot 'Noon-Chai',

What a blue water & blue sky was!

By: Imtiyaz Gull

Humanity Where Are You

Humanity Where are you?

We are being slathered!

Under your watchful eyes.

Why you turn your face away?

In Cashmere, we cry and cringe!

Look at me!

I would love to write verses about love.

Smell the scent of Pamposh,

I would love to close my eyes & see children smiling!

And playing a Tipcat,

No pellets pointing at their eyes.

I want to tell them 'Shal-Kaak' like stories in this peaceful land!

But we are sighing in Kashmir's alleyways!

We are crying & cringe!

Humanity! enough turning the other way,

Alas, our innocent children die!

By: Imtiyaz Gull

SOCIETY

Society is the Circle

Which locates only one center,

When passes a diameter, It becomes the semicircular

A colourful side and Black & White.

Where white is called the might

And he is always right!

Where black always fight

And never gets a right

Where people go on & on!

And they never realize that this is wrong.

Society you are the mighty wild!

Because you have destroyed so many child!

I hope the day shall surely come!

When we shall rise up as one!

By:Imtiyaz Gull

Our Saffron Land

There was a time of love & peace.

Our land had saffron, lofty pine trees.

Skies of blue & sunlit straights.

The moon was shining very bright.

The stars were twinkling with all their might.

Then Evils came in the human form.

Our Peaceful land in a deep black swarm.

No mercy have they by them side.

They pounce down and shattered lives.

Then prolonged cry through blackened Skies.

We ran but we couldn't hide.

Their daggers of death shines in our skies.

The plunge deep to Pierce our sunrise.

The darkness they spread their vengeful wings.

Our hearts now cracked our blood runs cold.

Our shroud of death they firmly fold.

The lofty mountains covered with snow.

Are hiding the blood, not letting it flow.

In darkness we die alone.

And the world turned to stone.

By: Imtiyaz Gull

Forgiveness And Repentance

Our presence is aimless & full of retrogress

Blackness surrounds us, we lay in distress

We running out of breath, & in despair

We take a deep breathe but feel no air

We experience a blackness inside & exhale

We thought we were powerful but now we are frail

Our body unload no sign of a soul

Messy & weeping, with no control

This departing soul cries loud of persecution

Making us comatose with no expression

O Almighty loosing you is the biggest fall

Without thou who can stand at all?

If one loses you,his existence dies

And He'll never rise!

O Allah! Who lost you
What did they find?

They did find only his Devils mind!

A revolution sharply begins to rise

Tears of repentance reach our eyes!

Now today is a good start

We are now enough smart!

Put right to a wrong

We have to be strong

May Almighty Allah give us a good sense

Forgive us & accept our repentance!

O Almighty Allah accept our repentance!

Neither it costs a cent nor amatter of expense

Hope & guidance with a heartfelt repentance

For a clear forbearance

Jannah is the place of acceptance

By: Imtiyaz Gull

Unexpressed Feelings

I love HER with profound affection & fondness,

Yet the love is still unexpressed.

The sweetness sings inside my heart,

But rarely lives inside my chest.

I ride a seesaw of sensations & passions,

My heart is filled with such dejections.

Unnerved I pen a love note,

Words that I have longed to say.

My words are vanishing,

And thoughts are melting.

My vision is blurring,

And mind is racing.

My heart is pounding,

Cause love is in the surrounding.

How can I explicit,
these unexpressed feelings?

I used to conceal them inside an envelope,

I wanna see that smile, it brings up.

Sometimes I looked at the sky,

And hurtle a cry!

These cries of mine,

Will never let me be fine!

I know you are Azeema!

And You will never let me on my Karma!

By: Imtiyaz Gull

A Dream Under The Chinar Tree

The zephyr stopped suddenly,

The blue sky turned into sunless sky,

Now their was no rain,

The crescent looked at me & disappeared,

Chinar leaves were drooping & crisping,

Branches wanted to cry but they were wood,

Then I cried and 'BOONI' comforts me,

I cried out: Innalaha Ma'Sabreen!

The chinar leaves fell over me,

And I asked, Why your leaves fell over me?

Reply was Allah's green signal gives me a pleasure!

Then I saw myself stood on a Peer Panjal,

A mountain overlooking me,

And the occupied land,

But I could see nothing!

It was dark, very dark

I wanted to see my homeland,

The Char-Chinar and Lotus in the Dal Lake,

The magical bubbling waterfall of AHARBAL,

I want to listen,

The Daroods and the Prayers,

And want to see:

The historical Masjid of the old city,

But I woke up,

No one awoke me up,

It was only a dream,

A tough and not yet fulfilled!

By: Imtiyaz Gull

Pandemic

You're Pandemic, You're Pandemic.

Your Infection grows an expiration.

You have come from Wuhan.

And have destroyed All Jahan

O Man! Your seven deadly Sins.

Ah! Allah has given you a comeuppance.

Because of your Avarice.

You became a bad choice.

Oh man! your lust

Giving you a dust!

Your Greed:

Is know your need!

Your Envy;

Has become your enemy!

Your Pride:

Is now your bad side!

O Man! You showed your ignorance.

And Almighty Allah showed His violence!

This Corona has only one solution.

That's do pray with a passion.

By: Imtiyaz Gull

We Who Lost The Paradise

We are gardens of Eden,

We who lost the paradise.

SHE expelled & killed us!

Under our Apple garden.

O land of ours remember us!

Wandering among the thrones of the Jungles.

Wandering in the rocky mountains,

In tumultuous cities & villages.

Diplomats followed us with their suspicious looks!

We dragged ourselves from place to place.

A day long memories of a reminiscences of home,

That yesterday, only yesterday were ours.

We don't care that we are tired,

Our hardened bodies are sleep deprived.

We are ceaseless,

And vigilant in our tasks.

We thrive on the mission,

And completing our objectives!

By: Imtiyaz Gull

My Beloved Mother

O mother! You brought me into this world.

Became my shield to the rain.

And thou can heal my every pain.

How blessed I was!

To your arms so warmly.

My very first sight,

Was the Noor shining Moon light

Despite my first cry

And thy worry, a sigh.

O mother! I don't deserve

I couldn't you preserve

Surely I don't deserve

A mother whom I should serve.

I remember your Pheran which you clad

Where I did something bad

Oh! How I pray my dear mother?

For a wish like no other.

Don't you see my dear mother?

Thy importance like no other

Oh! See the Surah al Ahqaf

You'll never do a Paap.

I grew to a child

And you was never a wild

When I did fall ill

Through a fever's chill

In thy arms, I did lay,

Until the night crept away

Oh mother! I shall always say

May you be happy in every way!

And so I beg for your mercy!

For I'm not a worthy.

By: Imtiyaz Gull

Unfortunate Victims

Defilers forced themselves on us.

We pleaded them to stop,

But they still wouldn't get off!

We closed our eyes tightly,

Wishing we were somewhere else!

Wishing someone had been here to help!

So what did they do?

They took us childhood away!

Our innocence and sense of security.

Alas! We were molested & zips on others mouth!

Were we that bad of girls?

Why were we auctioned with this demon to bid?

No one cares they said!

Throwed stone & we were dead!

The world screams 'Me Too'

How about a women too?

I can hear a cry of Parents!

Crying; O daughters We couldn't save you!

I hold a pen & wrote for unfortunate victims.

We are dead now,

So is the humanity!

By: Imtiyaz Gull

Kashmir is my elegy

Kashmir is my elegy,

And I am Her Poet.

Where Hunters are might,

And innocents try to hide,

Where students careers haven't bright,

For the right,

They always do fight!

But don't get their right.

I want to write,

But I have no right!

By: Imtiyaz Gull

Article 370

Thy name is Article three seventy

For the Kashmiris you were a dainty

To the politicians you provided a bounty

Now after abrogation,

You'll not provide more than a shanty

Thy begone will spoile my Kashmir's Canty!

You retrieve is peaceful Kashmir's only guarantee!

By: Imtiyaz Gull

LIBERTY

I get your pain & heeded to thy call

Innocent children & caring mothers I see you all!

O children of meadows stay strong!

For the day shall surely come,

When we shall rise up as one!

Mangled cadavers & rivers of blood,

Severed limbs lay on thy sanctified mud.

Upon which Awliya-e Kiram & martyrs stood

Pillars of faith & your forebears

Upholding all that is good!

Shall we laugh or cry at the irony?

That only the men of green place carry the bravery

That only the women of Caeshmeer bear the humanity!

That only the children of 'Pir-Vaer' posses the capacity!

To sacrifice & to provide liberty

Say; Phi Sabilil Lah, Phi Sabilil Lah!

We belong to Almighty Allah,

We belong to Almighty Allah!

Imtiyaz Gull

Aasifa Banoo An Unfortunate Victim

O Cruels thou forced yourself on me.

I pleaded thou to stop.

But you still wouldn't get off.

I closed my eyes tightly,

wishing I were somewhere else!

Wishing someone had been here to help!

O cruels! Thou forced yourself on me.

So what did they do?

They took my childhood away.

My innocence, my sense of security.

I was molested
Alas! zips on other mouths.

Was I that bad of a kid?

Why was I auctioned with this demon to bid?

No one cares, They said;

Threw stones, I was dead.

The world screams, “Me too”,

How about “A child too”?

A little girl of eight is raped.

I can hear the cries of the mother!

But she is just another Kashmiri

So did Asifa when they drugged her with

the pills.

I write for Asifa,

I hold a pen,

Asifa wasn't safe either.

Neither her Abbu Couldn't save her!

Nor her Ammi!

I am dead today,

And so is the humanity!

Imtiyaz Gull

Holy Masjid

Masjids were the shining light for all to see

Now are the darking light that we see!

A symbol of strength to the Muslim community

Today people made you infirmity!

The place to unite & prayer together

Now it has become a place denied together!

There was no Azaan echo throughout its dome

No love in our eyes & do disown!

Is it just a place, we often pass?

A holy place we once went, but now a place of past!

Our Holy Masjids are standing half empty

Now no longer a place of plenty!

People saying precautions are better than cure

But forget Salah is better then cure!

Don't gather and chat lowly on the streets

Come into the Masjid & make your obligation complete!

Perform Salah at Masjid follow Allah's command

Show the world our faith is glorious & grand!

Go to Masjid and be amongst those who care

Due to Corona don't feel fear!

By: Imtiyaz Gull

By: Imtiyaz Gull

My Proud And My Pride

O my beloved Kashmir!

Thou are my proud nation.
Core of my heart, my country!

You're naming the sweet Paradise on earth.

Almighty Allah has been bountiful to you,

Riches of value in every sphere.

The outside world's beauty is so limit,

When they heard, Kashmir is known as, "Paradise on earth!"

you're my proud, you're my pride,

Because you have given us so many gems!

Sheikh ul Aalam is known as 'Nund Reshi'

And Lal Ded is known as 'Lal Arifa'.

Nund Reshi and Lal Arifa,

Both have given us ma'rifa!

Core of my heart, my country!

I love my valley,

Of waterfalls & green jungles,

Of streams & Crystal like Kounsarnag!

Of meadows & Shepherd pastures crystal like rivulet.

I love your Dal Lake,

Your beauty & your nature's bounty,
The wide greenish land for me!

The unmatchable snow cliffs, looking like unbeatable Kashmir!

In the beauty and in the nature's bounty!

You're my proud, you're my pride!

Core of my heart, my country!

By: Imtiyaz Gull

Sonnet-I A Love Is Annoyed And The Love Is Feasted

'A love' is annoyed.

'The love' is feasted!

Metaphorical love is blind,

Bonafide love is gifted!

Thy metaphorical love ruined and tattered.

My Bonafide love gives me peace and tranquillity!

Thy lover always ordered,

My love gives me an equality!

Thy love has a lust.

My love is disciple of Almighty Allah!

And that's why thy love gives you a dust.

My love begins with Bis'millah!

Thy love has seven deadly sins.

O Almighty Allah absolves me of my sins!

By: Imtiyaz Gull

Sonnet-II Lovers Love And Haters Hate

Why lovers love has no fight?

And the haters hate has a wrath!

Let me compare lovers love to light.

And the haters hate is sloth.

Love is fruitful and insight!

Hate is lust, and da lust is short.

Love never says us to fight!

Love and hate are poles apart.

When you had a spiritual love, thou became Maulana Rumi!

Hate is hatred & maniac lust.

When your lover was God, thou became Maulana Jami!

Don't hate anyone, because it is dust.

Love getting ahead, it is never lost!

Hate is decline, it is ever lost.

By: Imtiyaz Gull

Limerick-IIGreenery And Scenery

Kashmir has a scenery,

SHE has full of greenery,

Kashmir is known as Paradise on earth!

And its my place of birth!

Allah has given HER, greatest scenery!

By: Imtiyaz Gull

The country has a post office but without postman

Shahid! When you had returned to this motherland

Muezzin was buried!

But that time people were scarce,

And some people exiled, became fugitive.

Now here is no muazzin and no adhan!

Those few also have been entombed

The Caesmeer is know robbed & our Ashiana are burnt!

Since that time, there is still no sun here, there is still no sun here!

How could we send our cries to you?

Because you are no more!

O Shahid! You sent countless cries, in form of letters.

I was not born, but now accept my thanks!

What else can I say? I don't want to live forever!

It snowing as I write this.Grief & sadness, I don't be brave.

You were Agha's Shahid,And that's why you were brave!

By: Imtiyaz Gull

Glossary

Prolonged Cry: As in grief or suffering.

Jungles: Forests.

Kahwa: It is a Kashmiri traditional preparation of green tea.

Noon Chai: Kashmiri traditional Salt tea.

Cashmere: It means Kashmir.

Pamposh: A lotus which grows in the Dal Lake (Kashmir).

Shal Kaak: Kashmiri word, means folk tales of Kashmir.

Sunlit Streets: receiving light from the sun.

Vengeful wings: To harm someone.

Kashmiri's alleyways: A narrow passage or lane of Kashmir.

Tipcat: A tapered piece of wood used in the game.

Azeema: Arabic word, which means greatness or nobility.

Chinar Tree: oriental plane.

Booni: oriental plane

Daroods: is an invocation which Muslims make by saying specific phrases to compliment the Prophet Muhammad(PBUH).

Innalaha Ma'Sabree: Holy Quran verse which means' "Surely, Allah is with those that are patient".

Pheran: A traditional kashmiri dress.

Paap: Hindi word, which means sin.

Pir-Vaer: The valley of saints.

Phi Sabilil Lah: An arabic verse, means: for the sake of Almighty Allah.

Awliya-e Kiram: Those who believe and they are always in fear.

Ma'rifa: Knowledge of spiritual truth.

Bis'millah: In the name of Allah.

Salah: Prayers, which Muslims offer in Mosque.

Dust: To cheat someone.

Char-Chinar: It is an island in the Dal Lake of Srinagar(Kashmir), surrounded by the chinar trees on all four sides of it.

Surah Al- Ahqaf: Al Ahqaf is the 46 chapter (Surah) of the Holy Quran.

www.ingramcontent.com/pod-product-compliance
Lightning Source LLC
LaVergne TN
LVHW050422160726
843469LV00041B/1199

* 9 7 8 9 3 5 5 5 9 1 4 9 4 *